OLD WHINE, NEW WINE

Encouragement to Slay the Week

K.M. ELLIS

Copyright © 2023 by K.M. Ellis

All rights reserved.

No part of this book may be reproduced in any form or by any electronic or mechanical means, including information storage and retrieval systems, without written permission from the author, except for the use of brief quotations in a book review.

And Fire Books
PO Box 223
Mt. Home, TN 37684

For Lucille.

"Peace does not dwell in outward things but within the soul; we may preserve it in the midst of the bitterest pain, if our will remains firm and submissive. Peace in this life springs from acquiescence to, not an exemption from, suffering."

— FRANÇOIS FÉNELON

CONTENTS

Introduction	ix
1. Sunny Sunday	1
Made to Be	2
2. Manic Monday	3
For Those in the Boat	4
3. Tune Up Tuesday	7
The Painful Process of Pruning	8
4. Reviving Wednesday	10
Real Mercy	11
5. Thirsty Thursday	13
Never Too Late	14
6. Fortifying Friday	16
The Battle: an allegory	17
7. Saturday Smatterday	21
Brokenness vs Freedom	22
8. Sunday, Someday	23
Beauty for Ashes	24
9. A Different Case of the Mondays	25
God is Our Coach	26
10. Tumultuous Tuesday	28
Knowing I AM	29
11. Winning on Wednesday	33
Thief of Joy, King of Pride	34
12. Thriving on Thursday	36
And So I Wait	37
13. Finishing on Friday	39
Unpreparedness	40
14. Something on Saturday	41
Belief is a Choice	42
15. Here Comes the Sun(day)	43
Divinely Found Pain	44
16. Monday Funday	45

Passing through the Waters	46
17. Seize the (Tues)day	48
The Pressure Reveals	49
18. Wednesday Schmensday	52
Lost My Marbles	53
19. Thirst Day, Thursday	56
The Wedding Dress	57
20. Fabulous Friday	60
The Tongue	61
21. Yay for Saturday	62
This Great Love	63
22. Sunday Kind of Love	65
An Encouraging Word	66
23. Monday Monday	67
The New Currency	68
24. Tuesday Fuse Day	70
The Complacency Trap	71
25. Rhyme & Reason Wednesday	76
Was Paul Really a Chauvinist?	77
26. Is Thursday a Terse Day?	82
You Are More	83
27. Friday No-Cry Day	87
A Bruised Reed	88
28. Saturday Musing	92
True Love	93
29. One Last Sunday	94
All that Saves	95
30. A Final Monday	97
The King's Gate	98
BONUS: Sneak Peek of Book #2	101
Two Wrongs	102
The Plight of Mankind	104
A Much-Needed Reminder	107
The Gift	108
About the Author	109

INTRODUCTION

Welcome to *Old Whine, New Wine: Encouragement to Slay the Week*. This isn't your typical devotional. Instead, you'll find a mix of devotions, poems, stories, prophetic words, and of course many words of encouragement in these pages.

The book was designed for quick, bite-sized morsels, perfect for people on-the-go who may not have time to read even one normal devotion during their busy day.

If that's you—or if you're simply looking for a little extra encouragement this season—you've come to the right place.

❧ 1 ❧
SUNNY SUNDAY

It's a Sunday, and this is the very first entry. Let's make it sunny…

MADE TO BE

God's call to repentance isn't a roadblock to keep you from being who you are. It's the avenue, the very Way, to become who you were made to be.

> *Jesus answered, "I am the way and the truth and the life. No one comes to the Father except through me."*
>
> — JOHN 14:6 (NIV)

2
MANIC MONDAY

In case you need a little extra encouragement to start the week...

FOR THOSE IN THE BOAT

Just because the storm comes doesn't mean you weren't supposed to get in the boat.

> *One day Jesus said to his disciples, "Let us go over to the other side of the lake." So they got into a boat and set out. As they sailed, he fell asleep. A squall came down on the lake, so that the boat was being swamped, and they were in great danger.*
>
> — LUKE 8:22-23 (NIV)

People are walking through fiery trials in this season. Many Christians are experiencing spiritual resistance, a type of invisible "pressure," that seems to be drawing them away from what the Lord has been calling them to do.

I hear prayer requests for Christians who are having sudden (and strange) health problems.

Godly couples, strong in the Lord, are having serious marriage problems.

The children of godly, loving parents are walking away from the Lord, seemingly overnight, and falling into traps involving sin, addiction, and false identities.

The leader of our summer mission team is experiencing uncountable distractions and odd situations at work, while two members of that same team have come under temptation to back out of the mission trip.

For the disciples (in Luke 8), this spiritual "pressure" manifested as a powerful squall while they were on their way to the Gerasenes. In their fear and distress, they may have regretted getting in that boat. Some of them likely assumed this was a *wrong place, wrong time* scenario.

But we know that's not true. Because Jesus is the one who told them to get in the boat.

Storms will come, but God has a plan. Trials may feel like chaos, but God is in control. We may be blindsided by these things, but Christ is not. He sees them coming, and He will work everything together for your good.

If God told you to get in the boat—whether that's your marriage, your children, your church, your mission, or whatever else—don't fret or worry, don't panic or doubt. Remember: you're crossing over, which means there *is* another side.

He is leading you through the storm. He is with you, so hang on. There is another side to this trial, to this storm, and He's our anchor through it.

> *The disciples went and woke him, saying, "Master, Master, we're going to drown!"*
>
> *He got up and rebuked the wind and the raging waters; the storm subsided, and all was calm. "Where is your faith?" he asked his disciples.*
>
> *In fear and amazement they asked one another,*

"Who is this? He commands even the winds and the water, and they obey him."

— LUKE 8:24-25 (NIV)

3
TUNE UP TUESDAY

A little extra *oomph* for your week...

THE PAINFUL PROCESS OF PRUNING

> *"He cuts off every branch in Me that bears no fruit, while every branch that does bear fruit He prunes so that it will be even more fruitful."*
>
> — JOHN 15:2 (NIV)

When pruning a plant, the gardener places his sheers to the branch and snips. *Ouch.* If the plant had feelings, it would surely cry out. Yet, we know this process is good for the plant because pruning causes a branch to bear more fruit.

But what does it look like when God, the Master Gardener, prunes the life of a Christian?

The Church is called to be a healing balm to a broken world. In order to bear fruit, our branches, our very lives, require pruning. Unfortunately, pruning is a painful process.

As humans, we recoil whenever we experience physical pain. In the same way, we often avoid mental and emotional pain by self-medicating with things like food or shopping, entertainment or social media—anything to help numb the hurt we're experiencing deep down in our hearts.

These are worldly coping mechanisms. The Christian life, however, is supposed to be different. We aren't called to avoid suffering. We're called to embrace it, to pick up our crosses and to follow Christ. Pain doesn't always come from God, but He certainly works all things—including the painful things—together for our good.

This enables us to bear more fruit. For His Glory. For His Kingdom.

Just as a grape must be crushed to make wine, as an olive must be pressed to produce oil, so, too, must the Christian endure a type of transformational crushing, a pressing, before the anointing flows.

The only way to get there—the only way to bear the sweet, life-giving fruit this broken world so desperately needs—is by abiding in the True Vine, Jesus Christ, and allowing Him to walk us through the painful process of pruning.

Let's pray this together: *Lord, I know I'm called to take up my cross like You did, but sometimes that hurts more than I can stand. Whatever trials I face, I need Your grace to endure so that I may bear much fruit. I'm asking in Jesus' name. Amen.*

4
REVIVING WEDNESDAY

It's the middle of the week. We need to be revived...

REAL MERCY

> *"You have heard that it was said, 'Eye for eye, and tooth for tooth.' But I tell you, do not resist an evil person. If anyone slaps you on the right cheek, turn to them the other cheek also."*
>
> — MATTHEW 5:38-39 (NIV)

God's law to the Jews is where "eye for an eye" comes from. This was to ensure that people who broke the law weren't punished beyond what was deserved (the punishment needed to fit the crime). The people, however, had been taking the law into their own hands, seeking vengeance to accomplish justice.

This is not the heart of God, and Jesus was correcting this wrong mindset in the Sermon on the Mount — not to say that the law was bad, but that people had taken it to a bad place in their hearts.

The law is for lawbreakers, lawlessness, and rebellion. As long as these things exist, laws (and the enforcement of them) are necessary. People are impacted more deeply by God's kindness — it's His kindness that leads us to repentance — and that kindness can take on different forms (someone receiving a lesser punishment than they deserve, for instance, but it can also look like someone serving the full sentence).

Sometimes the latter is what's really more merciful — for that person, for society, for the people who were wronged — but in a fallen world full of broken people (including judges, including prosecutors and juries, including us... everyone), what's best for all given parties is not easy to attain or even see. And so, there's injustice in the world.

What WE can do every single time is to forgive those who've transgressed us and ask for God's mercy over their lives. Turn the other cheek, as the Scriptures say. THAT is what Jesus was saying — not that the law should be abolished but that love fulfills the law.

> *But because of his great love for us, God, who is rich in mercy, made us alive with Christ even when we were dead in transgressions—it is by grace you have been saved.*
>
> — EPHESIANS 2:4-5 (NIV)

THIRSTY THURSDAY

We need Living Water to get through the week (drink up!)...

NEVER TOO LATE

It's never too late to get the ephod.

> *Then David said to Abiathar the priest, the son of Ahimelek, "Bring me the ephod." Abiathar brought it to him, and David inquired of the Lord, "Shall I pursue this raiding party? Will I overtake them?"*
>
> *"Pursue them," he answered. "You will certainly overtake them and succeed in the rescue."*
>
> — 1 SAMUEL 30:7-8 (NIV)

When David was an outlaw and was forced to live among the Philistines, he settled in a town called Ziklag. One day, David and his men returned to Ziklag to find their homes destroyed, their women and children kidnapped.

The Amalekites had raided Ziklag while David and his men had been away.

I had my own Ziklag moment recently. While my husband and I were away, some people used our rental as a crashpad and drughouse. The police said we were lucky. Fentanyl is rampant, and a miniscule amount left behind on a counter or table would have been deadly had we come into contact with it.

I was shocked and angry. I felt violated.

As I prayed, the Lord pointed me to the story of Ziklag. David surely felt angry, too. I could imagine he felt violated, perhaps even helpless. The man was in a crisis—a full-on, full-fledged crisis—and what was his response?

Did he complain to his friends?

Did he insist this wasn't fair?

Did he fall into depression?

Did he numb his mind/heart or check out mentally?

We've all responded in such ways before. It's human nature. There have even been times when I've felt like God didn't care, like He had "let" something bad happen to me. If ever there was someone who had a chance to feel this way, it was David at Ziklag—and yet, this was not his response.

Instead, David determined he would seek the LORD, and he did. Because he understood it's never too late to get the ephod.

Are you in a crisis? Maybe you're struggling and feel like no one can help. I'm here to tell you God is able. He has wisdom for the most complicated situation. He gives hope when things seem most hopeless.

Pray this prayer with me: *Father God, You're the One who declares the end from the beginning, and I need Your help now—real, practical help like You gave David at Ziklag. I'm asking in Jesus's name.*

6
FORTIFYING FRIDAY

The LORD is a Strong Tower. Whom shall I fear?

THE BATTLE: AN ALLEGORY

The weight of my sword pulls my hands toward the ground. I tighten my grip, armor clanking, and step onto the battlefield. My breastplate is heavy. My belt is cinched so tightly it digs into the curves of my waist.

I peer out from beneath my helmet.

An enemy hoard kicks up dust in the distance. The stench of death, as thick as the darkness from whence it comes, rolls off their army like smoke rolls off a burning building.

Moisture pours down my face. I widen my stance and take in my surroundings. Empty battlefield stretches around me, and fear drains the strength from my knees. Fellow soldiers should be here. We're supposed to fight this battle together.

Dread tiptoes through me. How can I accomplish the mission by myself? I need support troops. Without them, I'm exposed, vulnerable.

I envision my Fortress. It's my place of refuge, of safety, and a contingency plan forms in the back of my mind. If I cannot stand my ground, I know where to go.

The hoard draws closer.

I swing my sword—a test swing, and not a very good one.

I stagger and nearly topple over. Anxiety grips me until I can no longer breathe. A jolt of panic sends tremors through my legs and arms, even into my hands.

I turn and flee.

The metal casings around my feet and shins—special shoes I'm required to wear for battle—clank as I dash across the battlefield. Hot air rushes over my face. In the distance, a stone tower reaches into the sky.

My Fortress.

I turn my attention on the entrance—or where the entrance *should* be. Smooth, gray stones cover the spot. My thoughts swirl. Where is the door?

My attention travels upward, following the gray stones to the top. I circle around the structure. There are no windows or doors anywhere. It's as if all means of entry have vanished.

I cannot escape. Which means I must now face my enemy.

The hoard arrives. Three enemy troops break away, swords drawn. I pivot. Their eyes smolder red—hot coals burning in demonic skulls—and my armor grows unbearably heavy. Sweat slicks my forehead. My helmet slides around.

I push the helmet up, brain buzzing with panicked thoughts and potential scenarios, none of which are good. Moisture coats my palms until my sword feels like a wet bar of soap.

The soldiers stalk forward, growling, flashing their fangs. They rear back, swords raised. I brace myself as the blades crash down on me. Metal clangs. Flesh and bone ache, bruising beneath my armor.

The briefest of respites arrives between blows. I regain my footing, push out a breath, and counterattack. The soldiers weave in and out as I swing my sword.

Swish. The blade cuts air.

Swish-swish. Swish. I strike nothing. My arm muscles quiver.

Sunlight glints off the steel blades raised against me. Fierce determination glimmers in my enemy's eyes. The troops deliver their next blows.

Clang! The swords connect, harder this time. I topple sideways. "Help me." My voice hitches. "Where are You?"

I'm here.

The voice is sure, unmistakable—and yet, forged steel continues clashing against my breastplate, my arm coverings, my helmet. I collapse, and the swords rain down on me. Each blow sends pain roaring through my body.

"I need You. Please." Tears pluck my eyes. Panic chokes my voice. "Where are You?"

I'm here, He says again. But the attack continues.

The blows intensify, merciless and seemingly without end. The pain crushes the air from my lungs. My body aches, weakening. I must act now. If I don't, I may die.

I push myself up and try once more to stave off the attack. The effort is shallow—too little, too late. The soldiers scream, a battle cry so fierce it rattles my armor. Nay, my very being.

The troops converge and deliver a powerful blow that lifts me off my feet and sends me flying through the air.

Thud.

I land on my back, dust pluming. My sword clatters to the ground. My breastplate tears away. One of my shoes falls off, and my belt has broken loose. My helmet is the only piece of armor that remains intact.

But where is your shield?

I wince and lift my head. Where *is* my shield? I never had it for the battle.

The enemy suddenly withdraws. Something, some unseen force, is keeping the troops at bay. They growl, snapping at me, eager to devour the fleshy heart beating in my chest—a heart now exposed because my breastplate has fallen off.

I gather my armor and sword and limp to my Fortress. The door appears and opens before me. I step inside, slam the door shut, and shove the lock into place.

My arms quiver as I carry everything up the winding staircase. The sound of steel scraping stone echoes through the stairwell. Blood leaks down my face and splatters the stone steps. Hot tears sting the wounds on my cheeks.

I enter the chamber of my Sanctuary, dropping everything in a heap on the floor, and trudge across the room. The window is precisely where it's supposed to be. Why couldn't I see it earlier? Had fear blinded me, kept me from entering my Fortress?

I lean out the window and peer down. My enemy hisses at me from far below, their eyes red and fiery. Curses and a darkness most foul spray from their jowls.

My heart trembles within me. I wasn't prepared for what happened in battle, the viciousness and cunning my enemy delivered.

I wasn't, but I will be.

7
SATURDAY SMATTERDAY

You might be winding down (or up). Either way, let's take a moment (a teeny, tiny second) to sit at the feet of Jesus...

BROKENNESS VS FREEDOM

Here's a word for all of us, something to keep in mind...something to remember:

Brokenness breeds brokenness. But freedom births freedom.

> *It is for freedom that Christ has set us free. Stand firm, then, and do not let yourselves be burdened again by a yoke of slavery.*
>
> — GALATIANS 5:1 (NIV)

8
SUNDAY, SOMEDAY

Relax. Take a break. Have a Sunday "Sabbath."
Whatever you do, rest in Him...

BEAUTY FOR ASHES

Those who sow with tears
Will reap with songs of joy
Those who go out weeping
Shall return and shall enjoy
They're carrying their sheaves with them
They're carrying a song
The pain is gone forever
And they're singing all day long
Mourning turns to dancing
Depression turns to song
He takes the old and broken things
And breaks them 'til they're strong
Ashes turn to beauty
And my old-self fades away
A brand new song for us to sing
A hopeful, peaceful day

— K.M. ELLIS

… 9 …

A DIFFERENT CASE OF THE MONDAYS

Here we go again. Let's do this thing…

GOD IS OUR COACH

I played the Deep Deck game with God, and He answered.

> *Beloved, don't be surprised at the fiery trial when it comes upon you to test you, as though something strange were happening....*
>
> — 1 PETER 4:12 (NIV)

While I was on a mission trip, one of my teammates made something called a Deep Deck—a deck of playing cards with handwritten questions. When we wanted to go deeper with someone, that person drew a card and answered the question. Questions included: *What are your gifts?* Or: *What does your dream vacation look like?*

One day I drew a Deep Deck card for Jesus, thinking it would be neat to go deeper with my Savior. The question I drew: *What's your dream job?* I didn't know how Jesus would respond. Doesn't He already have His dream job? He is a King, after all.

I prayed anyway, asking Him to somehow, in some way, answer.

My mission team organized a family film night where we showed *Facing the Giants*. In it, Coach Taylor makes Brock (the star athlete) do a drill called the Death Crawl, but he had to do it blindfolded, carrying a teammate on his back.

The coach speaks encouragement, walking beside Brock who's death-crawling across the field. Brock has promised to do his best—his *very best*—and Coach Taylor holds him to it.

Tears pooled in my eyes as I watched Brock crawl yard after yard—despite his arms burning, despite his strength waning—but Coach Tayler believed in Brock and said to keep going: past the twenty-yard line, past the fifty.

He wouldn't let Brock quit until his player collapsed...in the end-zone.

This is a picture of God working with us. When we think we can't take another step, He says, "Keep going." He brings us to our limits, walking beside us through trials while conforming us to the image of His Son.

In this way, God is like a coach—and that's when it dawned on me. I had asked God about His dream job when I drew the Deep Deck card!

(Hear me out—I'm *not* saying the God of Heaven and Earth is lining up for a coaching gig at UT, but I do think, in His way, this was His answer.)

Has God asked you to go farther than you thought you could go? Have you ever felt like you're going through fire?

Let's pray this together: *God, I realize fiery trials are supposed to refine us by burning off the impurities. It's a good process, but a painful one, and sometimes it's too much to bear. Give me the grace to endure. Don't let me give up. In Jesus' name. Amen.*

10

TUMULTUOUS TUESDAY

Are you having a rough week? Here's a pick-me-up.
Having a great week? Let's make it even better...

KNOWING I AM

Knowing I AM means knowing *who* I am.

> *Moses said to God, "Suppose I go to the Israelites and say to them, 'The God of your fathers has sent me to you,' and they ask me, 'What is his name?' Then what shall I tell them?"*
>
> *God said to Moses, "I AM WHO I AM. This is what you are to say to the Israelites: 'I AM has sent me to you.'"*
>
> — EXODUS 3:13-14 (NIV)

I had a dream I was struggling with sin. I didn't know what the sin was, but I felt empty inside. Empty, yet also weighed down. I couldn't explain how I knew any of this, but I said to someone, "I know it's idolatry."

The scene changed. I was at my church, and our worship team was singing "Take Your Place" by John Thurlow. I had a revelation about the lyrics, which talks about Jesus being at the center of our hearts, and when I woke up, I heard my pastor's wife singing the song. Then this word came to me:

"There's a disconnect in your heart/mind/spirit, like pieces of a puzzle that are supposed to be connected by another (missing) piece. You can see the two pieces—you recognize them, you can identify them—but you don't yet have the missing piece to connect them. God is going to connect the disconnect. He's going to give you the missing piece."

Shortly thereafter, I heard a sermon about something called an "orphan spirit." This spirit operates through rejection and abandonment, causing us to not know our fathers. The absence of an earthly father then creates a disconnect in understanding our Heavenly Father.

Since we lack this framework in the seen realm, the framework in the unseen realm is faulty or damaged, possibly nonexistent. Even when we become Christians, we might experience extreme fear because we don't really believe we're protected.

God is trustworthy. He is our defender and strong tower, but sometimes—when we've been under the influence of an orphan spirit our entire lives—we only know God as protector in our minds. We don't really know it down in our hearts.

As I listened to this sermon, I realized the lesson coincided with the dreams I'd had. This was the disconnect I was experiencing—to believe in my mind that God was my Father, and therefore my protector, but not believe it down in my heart. Instead, my need for safety (to *feel* safe, even if that feeling was an illusion) had become an idol.

It had taken the center place in my heart, the place only God should have.

Ty Gibson of Light Bearers says this:

> *Fatherhood is an identity-shaping vocation. Whether he does so consciously or not, a dad tells his child who and what to become. The child is significantly defined by the father's manner of relating to him. By his actions and attitudes toward the child, the father projects an identity onto the child so that he grows up to think and feel about himself according to the father's enacted vision of him. Day-by-day, hour-by-hour, a bequeathing of character occurs in the fathering process. The child comes to see himself or herself through daddy's eyes.*

To sum it up: *The child will inevitably become whatever the father projects* (Gibson, Light Bearers).

Spiritually speaking, I always think of my identity in terms of "me," who I am, who God made me to be. But the pastor giving this sermon spoke about our identity in terms of who *God* is.

I know God as Father. I call Him Dad all the time. But even though I've known my identity is found in Him, I guess I still saw these things as separate: His identity and mine.

Two separate pieces.

But God actually *imparts* identity to me *because* of who He is. Therefore, I can't truly know who I am if I don't truly know who *He* is.

Knowing I AM means knowing *who* I am.

So how do I overcome the things that have been overcoming me? How do I stand firm and fear not as God commands 365 times throughout the Bible? How do I believe, truly believe, what He says when everything around me says I'm unloved, unsafe, unprotected, uninvited, un-everything?

How do I come under a protection I was always supposed

to have but never did from my biological father (and therefore don't recognize when I see it in my Heavenly Father)?

How?

By knowing Him. Because...

Knowing I AM means knowing *who* I am.

> "I am the good shepherd; I know my sheep and my sheep know me—just as the Father knows me and I know the Father—and I lay down my life for the sheep."
>
> — JOHN 10:14-15 (NIV)

11
WINNING ON WEDNESDAY

This is my declaration: the victory is ours in Christ...

THIEF OF JOY, KING OF PRIDE

> *Pride goes before destruction, a haughty spirit before a fall.*
>
> — PROVERBS 16:18 (NIV)

Do you ever notice how the world's way of encouraging someone oftentimes requires tearing down somebody else? I'm not talking about an angry reaction, lashing out. I'm not even talking about general criticism.

If a person is down and their friend tries to encourage them, they do it—not by lifting that person up, but by tearing another person down. Why? Because comparison gives them a way to say, "At least I'm better than this other person. At least I'm not as bad."

But comparison isn't just the thief of joy, as some say. It's the king of pride. Pride uses things like comparison to make us feel better about ourselves when, in reality, we've all sinned, we've all fallen short of the glory of God.

None of us are better than anyone. Only God is good.

Only He is just. Only He is wise. At the foot of the cross, we're all on even ground.

> *When pride comes, then comes disgrace, but with humility comes wisdom.*
>
> — PROVERBS 11:2 (NIV)

12

THRIVING ON THURSDAY

The thief came to steal, kill, and destroy. Jesus came to give us life abundant. Today, let's *choose* to choose life…

AND SO I WAIT

This is what Yahweh says: "This is My command—be strong and courageous! Do not be afraid or discouraged. For the Lord your God is with you wherever you go."

I say: But I don't know how. How can I be strong and courageous when my enemies surround me—the people I thought were my friends? When they were ill, I put on sackcloth and humbled myself with fasting. When my prayers returned to me unanswered, I went about mourning as though for my friend or brother. I bowed my head in grief as though weeping for my mother.

But when I stumbled, they gathered in glee; assailants gathered against me without my knowledge. How can I not be discouraged or afraid? I don't know how to be strong and courageous in the midst of such betrayal.

He responds: "I took you from the ends of the earth, from its farthest corners I called you. I said, 'You are my servant'; I have chosen you and have not rejected you. So do not fear, for I am with you; do not be dismayed. For I am the

Lord your God who takes hold of your right hand and says to you, 'Do not fear; I will help you.'"

Weeping and broken, I ask: How long, Lord, must I call for help, but you do not listen? Or cry out to you, "Violence!" but you do not save? Why do you make me look at injustice? Why do you tolerate wrongdoing?

I have navigated lies perpetrated against me. I stepped into traps that had been strategically hidden, and I was lured into them from many sides. When I stayed silent, I was mocked and bullied. When I spoke out, all sought vengeance against me.

I'm sick in my spirit. My heart is shattered. I do not know what to do—but my eyes are on You.

13
FINISHING ON FRIDAY

When we're weak, He is strong.
Let's finish this week strong in Him...

UNPREPAREDNESS

Unpreparedness is a weight other people are forced to bear. When I show up unprepared, the people around me suffer.

> *Stand firm then, with the belt of truth buckled around your waist, with the breastplate of righteousness arrayed, and with your feet fitted with the readiness of the gospel of peace.*
>
> — EPHESIANS 6:14-15 (NIV)

14
SOMETHING ON SATURDAY

Monday thru Friday may be the "grind," but we have obligations during the weekend, too. Commit it all to Him...

BELIEF IS A CHOICE

The Holy Spirit says: "Belief is a choice."

He is not here to "convince" or "persuade" you of something. He won't try to control what you think.

Instead, He shows people the truth and lets them decide if they will believe it. He helps them and teaches them, unveiling hidden things—but, ultimately, He allows us to decide for ourselves if we will believe Him.

That's free will, and it's very important to Him. He wants people to believe because they choose to, not because they feel forced or obligated to.

> *"But if serving the LORD seems undesirable to you, then choose for yourselves this day whom you will serve, whether the gods your ancestors served beyond the Euphrates, or the gods of the Amorites, in whose land you are living. But as for me and my household, we will serve the LORD."*
>
> — JOSHUA 24:15 (NIV)

15

HERE COMES THE SUN(DAY)

Sundays can rock, even if the rest of the week doesn't...

DIVINELY FOUND PAIN

Integral, whimsical
Everything's flimsy, though
Blinding, not binding
I'm sad, but I'm finding
That suffering isn't
The worst kind of rhyme scheme
It isn't so fearful
It isn't so frightening
Divine Intervention
Are you paying attention?
Divinely found pain
In the grand scheme of things
A vapor, a breath
Is but all we have left
But it's never enough
When we're holding our breath

— K.M. ELLIS

16
MONDAY FUNDAY

Fuel for your Monday endeavors...

PASSING THROUGH THE WATERS

Have you ever had one of those mornings where nothing seems to go right? You find yourself making entire lists of mistakes, and all you can think is:

I'm a screw up.
I can't get anything right.
Yesterday was okay, but today I'm crying my eyes out.

This was how I felt recently, on a day when my rearview mirror seemed to be full of regrets. Then I opened my Bible app, and this was the verse of the day....

> *"When you pass through the waters, I will be with you; and when you pass through the rivers, they will not sweep over you. When you walk through the fire, you will not be burned; the flames will not set you ablaze."*
>
> — ISAIAH 43:2 (NIV)

After I read this, something occurred to me.

God didn't say there wouldn't be any rivers to cross. He said He wouldn't allow the waters to sweep me away.

He didn't promise that I would never have to walk through fire. He promised that I wouldn't be burned and set ablaze.

In other words, trials are going to come, but when I trust in His wisdom and strength, His great love, He will make a way because He is with me.

That gives me so much comfort. I hope it does for you, too.

Let's agree together: *God, You are trustworthy, and we trust in Your love and grace to get us through this day. We choose to trust that You will see us through the challenges and the trials, and we ask You to make known Your peace, the peace of Jesus Christ. Amen.*

17

SEIZE THE (TUES)DAY

Carpe diem is Latin for "seize the day."
Let's slay the week by seizing this day...

THE PRESSURE REVEALS

"Ew, Lord. *That* was in my heart?"

> *Jesus said, "Father, forgive them, for they do not know what they are doing."*
>
> — LUKE 23:34 (NIV)

A person's goodness isn't determined by how he or she acts when everything is going right. It's determined when everything is going wrong. Life is putting the squeeze on people, myself included, and a lot of junk is bubbling up.

The process isn't pretty, and I wanted to understand why it's necessary. Why would God want us to experience things that bring out the worst in us?

First, I think it's important to recognize our behavior. How do we react when we're not feeling loved or appreciated by our spouse? What about when we're stressed because of work, children, or finances? We want to be led by the Spirit, but if we're struggling—I mean, really struggling—isn't it natural to walk in the flesh?

It is for me.

When I'm feeling the squeeze of life, any number of negative feelings and behaviors rise to the surface, and they're all quite natural—complaining, negativity, being short-tempered. I overeat and overindulge, turning to worldly outlets for relief—shopping, social media, entertainment—and it all seems justifiable in the moment.

Then I decided to examine how Jesus handled stress during His ministry.

When He was exhausted, He acted in kindness. When He was tempted, He chose high honor. When He wanted to rest but people needed a touch from God, He had compassion on them. When He was betrayed, He trusted in His father and pressed on with the mission.

People wrongfully accused Jesus throughout the Gospels, yet He always spoke the truth in love. Sometimes, He didn't speak at all. He simply remained quiet. And as He hung on the cross, He said, "Father, forgive them, for they know not what they do" (Luke 23:34).

When Jesus suffered the most—a suffering He anticipated with such dread that He sweated blood—*forgiveness* welled up in His heart. He didn't self-medicate. He didn't turn to vices. Someone offered Him wine mixed with gall (a sedative to numb the excruciating pain), but He refused.

Instead, He continued to rely on His Father, and He remained obedient unto death. Even death on a cross.

It's possible for people to lead decent lives under the right conditions. We can help others. We can do good works. If, however, the wrong conditions befall us—and they will, eventually—the pressure unmasks our true nature. This is true for

THE PRESSURE REVEALS

all people, and we find shadows of this truth throughout God's creation.

Picture a peach. If this peach is fresh and ripe, what leaks out when we squeeze it? Fresh, sweet juice, of course. That's what happened when the world applied pressure to Jesus. The goodness and faithfulness of God poured forth from Him.

If that peach is rotten—well, rotten juice leaks out. That's what happens when life applies pressure to *us*. This isn't a mark of how "bad" we are (all have sinned and fallen short of the glory of God, right?). This is a mark of how deep God's love is—that He would desire to be in relationship with us, despite our fallen nature.

Jesus said, "For if you love those who love you, what reward do you have? Do not even the tax collectors do the same?" (Matthew 5:46). God's character shines through in that while we were yet sinners, while we were yet enemies of God, Christ died for us.

We all have bad moments. We miss the mark. We become discouraged, even disheartened. Can you think of a time like this where God's kindness showed up? Perhaps you hit a low point, and a friend called to encourage you. Perhaps a financial crisis struck, and the funds showed up at the right moment.

Whatever it was, reflect on that moment. Let's pray this psalm together.

> *Remember, Lord, your great mercy and love, for they are from of old. Do not remember the sins of my youth and my rebellious ways; according to Your love remember me, for You, Lord, are good.*
>
> — PSALM 25:6-7 (NIV)

18
WEDNESDAY SCHMENSDAY

How's your week going? Blah? Time to turn things around...

LOST MY MARBLES

I lost my marbles when I met Jesus.

> *"Come to Me, all you who are weary and burdened, and I will give you rest."*
>
> — MATTHEW 11:28 (NIV)

Sin had carved a path of destruction in my life, putting me in dangerous situations and leading into many hardships. I'd come to be proud of my brokenness, all this baggage I'd been carrying around. I called myself strong, a survivor.

Then God revealed the truth about this baggage through a metaphor He showed me.

In the metaphor, I saw myself collecting marbles, storing them in a sack, and then dragging them around everywhere I went. These marbles represented my greatest achievements, my biggest failures, the many ways I had struggled, and all of my most harrowing tales.

I thought these marbles had value, so I'd been holding on to them, hoping I might be able to cash them in someday. Eventually, one sack wasn't enough to hold all them all. I had multiple sacks, and the load was so heavy—but I kept dragging them around everywhere I went.

The day came where my baggage became too burdensome. My health had deteriorated. Friends had betrayed me. I had accrued tremendous debt—financial debt I owed to the bank and inner debt that left me feeling bankrupt.

I tried making new friends. They treated me worse than the old ones.

I applied to a Master's program in England. I was accepted, but I couldn't afford the visa.

I entered a writing competition, submitting the most inspiring story I'd ever written: *my* story, of how I'd acquired all my marbles. I didn't even get an honorable mention.

"But look how valuable this is!" I would say to people as I reached into one of my heavy sacks (still in this metaphor). "This marble represents the friends who've used and abused me. And this!" I pulled out a different marble. "This represents all the traveling I've done! It means I'm knowledgeable and cultured!"

I showcased my most heart-wrenching tragedies—like the house fire I'd survived and the abusive relationships I'd been in. These marbles were near and dear to my heart. But I began to realize they meant little to other people.

Disillusionment crushed me. I'd been lugging around these marbles, thinking—*believing*—the world wanted them, that people would give me something in return for them: attention, affirmation, acceptance. I would've settled for a little sympathy.

I got nothing. Nobody wanted my marbles. They were worthless.

But there was one Person who cared about my marbles, who'd been there each time I had collected one—whenever I'd experienced a heartache or tragedy, whenever I'd survived a situation or been cast off by the world.

His name is Jesus. When I gave my life to Him, He gave me eternal life and a way—a real, actual way—to unload these marbles I'd found myself stuck with. They weren't valuable (not really), but He paid the ultimate price for them. He paid for them with His life.

Will you pray this with me? *Lord, You promised to carry my burdens. If I burden myself with marbles, thinking they give me value, remind me of the truth: they're just marbles, and only You, the Eternal One, can redeem me. In Jesus' name. Amen.*

19
THIRST DAY, THURSDAY

Let's reflect on this, along with today's encouragement (next page), as we go about our day...

> *On the last day of the feast, the great day, Jesus stood up and cried out, "If anyone thirsts, let him come to me and drink. Whoever believes in me, as the Scripture has said, 'Out of his heart will flow rivers of living water.'"*

— JOHN 7:37-38 (NIV)

THE WEDDING DRESS

It's not easy planning a wedding, but the plans for mine went seamlessly. Well, except for one thing. My wedding dress.

> *And I saw the holy city, New Jerusalem, coming down out of heaven from God, prepared as a bride adorned for her husband.*
>
> — REVELATION 21:2 (NIV)

I once had a dream where I saw myself in a wedding dress. It was beautiful: strapless, sparkly, with a curvy sweetheart neckline. A year later, I was engaged and went looking for that dress.

The first bridal shop had one remarkably similar. The problem? They could only sell me the sample dress, which looked like it'd been tried on by a thousand other brides-to-be. The store also wouldn't budge on the $1300 price tag.

My fiancé and I couldn't squeeze that into our budget, so

I went online and did some research. Soon, I found the exact same dress, pre-owned, for $700...except that when I received it, mere weeks before the wedding, I realized it wasn't the same dress at all. The designer had used polyester instead of satin, and the color was a hideous yellow-ivory instead of sparkling white.

It was also too tight, despite the fact that I'd lost weight.

Panic gripped me. I sent the faux dress back, rushed to the bridal shop, and begged them to sell me the sample dress. "We're happy to do that," the clerk had said, "but the dress still needs a lot of work."

She was right. The beading and stitching were coming apart, and the dress itself was dirty from being handled so much. Not only would the dress need to be professionally cleaned, it required a lot of repair work that could only be done by a tailor or seamstress—and it was all going to cost extra with the rush delivery fees.

I was running out of time and agreed to buy the dress as-is. I paid full price, and then I set out to make the dress ready-to-wear by my wedding day. Turns out, I underestimated what it would take to do that.

Having the dress professionally cleaned cost a whopping $220, so I had to pinch pennies on the needed tailoring. I used a woman well-known for having affordable rates, but by the time she finished, the dress still needed a ton more work.

I then took the dress to another lady, a seamstress who specialized in wedding gowns. These bills combined came to $250.

I couldn't believe it. If I'd bought the dress new, it would have cost $1300. This worn, dirty sample dress was costing me nearly $2000!

My fiancé and his family were appalled. They wanted me to return the dress, saying it wasn't worth it and that we'd figure out something else.

Ultimately, I couldn't bring myself to do that. Yes, we were running out of time, but this was also the dress God wanted me to have. I felt sure of it.

"Help me understand," I prayed. "I thought this was the dress from my dream—so then, why is everything going wrong?"

What I didn't realize was that He had been using these things to reveal more of Himself, more of His great love, because the wedding dress...was me.

The Lord once had a vision of me, beautiful, sparkling, and brand new. But when He found me, I was filthy, worn, and falling apart. I'd been made grimy by the world, by people who'd failed me—like my father, who abandoned me, and all the men who'd used me. My heart required intricate repair, and my dirty, soiled soul badly needed to be cleaned.

I wasn't worth the price it would cost to do that, but God saw the beauty that *could* be, the beauty of something He dearly loved, so He paid full price for me with the precious blood of His only Son.

Once He had me, He invested a tremendous amount of time and effort, caring for me, fixing me up, and tending to all the broken parts of me. He revealed Himself as a Master Tailor, and my new life in Him was His masterpiece.

Let's pray this together: *Lord, I'm not worth much to the world. People have cheered when I've fallen, celebrating my failures, and I can't count the number of times I've been rejected.*

But Your love, God, is forever. You've promised to never forsake me. You've said that even if my own mother and father reject me, You would not reject me. You're gracious and kind, long-suffering—Jesus, You are worthy of ALL praise.

Make me ready for Your return, as a bride adorned for her Husband. I ask in Jesus' name. Amen.

❧ 20 ☙
FABULOUS FRIDAY

You worked hard this week. Finish strong...

THE TONGUE

The power of life and death is in the tongue.

So then, what am I speaking over myself and, more importantly, over others? How am I using my words? To build up? To tear down? I'm called to edify others, but am I doing it?

I should ask myself these things every single day, with everything I say. That would be incredibly challenging, but there's tremendous wisdom in pausing to reflect before we speak.

> *The tongue also is a fire, a world of evil among the parts of the body. It corrupts the whole body, sets the whole course of one's life on fire, and is itself set on fire by hell.*
>
> — JAMES 3:6 (NIV)

21

YAY FOR SATURDAY

We made it. Praise the Lord!

THIS GREAT LOVE

My heart is breaking
Tenderly
Gently o'er the
Rolling seas
Gently and with
Perfect ease
In this great Love
You have for me

Break my heart, Lord
Perfectly
Whispering
You speak to me
Singing, slowly
Shaping me
In this great Love
You have for me

Touch my heart
So mercifully

Draw me out
O'er stormy seas
Draw me out — say:
"Come to Me."
For if I fall, You'll
Carry me

In Your great love
God, do not wait
Please don't ever
Hesitate
For I may doubt
And I may faint
And I might pause
With shaky faith

But I can fight
I will not sink
I will not run
Nor overthink
I will not shun
Nor push, nor flee

From this great love
You have for me

— K.M. ELLIS

22
SUNDAY KIND OF LOVE

It's a grand day to reconnect with friends and family (and our Heavenly Father!)...

AN ENCOURAGING WORD

"Almost" isn't good enough.

He is jealous for you, and He won't stop pursuing you until you belong completely to Him. He wants to show you what real love is, and I'm so incredibly excited to see what He is going to do in your life.

23
MONDAY MONDAY

Fresh week. Fresh start...

THE NEW CURRENCY

> *"And then shall many be offended, and shall betray one another, and shall hate one another."*
>
> — MATTHEW 24:10 (NIV)

If it seems like there's no end in sight when it comes to cancel culture, that's because there isn't. There will always be more things, more people, more products and brands to be canceled because people have a vested interest in this process.

Although these people espouse values like kindness, they are (in reality) climbing a metaphoric ladder and competing for the limited resources available at each rung. It's a cutthroat world, and anyone who's higher up on the ladder is fair game.

(This is why you'll often see the cancelers themselves getting canceled. The people on the lower rungs have to tear down those above them in order to make room for their own ambitions.)

> *Jesus replied, "Very truly I tell you, everyone who sins is a slave to sin."*
>
> — JOHN 8:34 (NIV)

Offense has become a commodity. It's practically a currency at this point, and people have become enslaved to it in much the same way other people are enslaved to things like money, greed, drugs, and sex.

And because these people's livelihoods are dependent on other people (as many as possible) being offended *with* them, they absolutely must spread that offense, causing others to take up offense on behalf of causes and people.

> *A man's discretion makes him slow to anger, and it is his glory to overlook a transgression.*
>
> — PROVERBS 19:11 (NIV)

During a time when everyone is looking for reasons to be angry, what if we, as believers, look for reasons to be thankful? Instead of looking for reasons to be offended, what if we look for reasons to forgive?

Because offense may be the new currency on Earth, but mercy is a treasure stored up in Heaven.

> *"The heart is deceitful above all things and beyond cure. Who can understand it? I the Lord search the heart and examine the mind, to reward each person according to their conduct, according to what their deeds deserve."*
>
> — JEREMIAH 17:9-10 (NIV)

24
TUESDAY FUSE DAY

Did your fuse get snuffed out?
Let's relight it. We have a week to slay...

THE COMPLACENCY TRAP

Complacency (*n*) – a feeling of contentment or self-satisfaction, especially when coupled with an unawareness of danger, trouble, or controversy. See also *self-congratulation*, *gratification*, and *pride*.

I've been struggling spiritually. I want to live a Spirit-filled life, but the truth is, I'm not in the Word nearly enough. Even meditating on a short verse would be great, yet I can't seem to do that simple thing on a regular basis.

As I've been pondering this, I've recalled times I was zealous about something—where I was passionate, motivated, and very much dedicated—but then my zeal faded. Even losing weight has been a huge struggle. I get motivated to do the workouts and eat right, but my motivation inevitably wanes.

I begin to feel like I "deserve" a reward, that I've earned it, but too many treat meals reverse my results and render my hard work useless.

I sat down one evening, frustrated and confused. I knew

what to do, but I couldn't seem to do it. Why? The answer evaded me, so I prayed. The word "complacency" came to my mind.

I've never thought much about complacency. Whenever I've failed in any of the above areas, I've always repented of things like apathy, unfaithfulness, lack of self-control, being too satisfied, being too willing to give up.

The biggest one of all? Laziness. This might be spiritual (e.g., not praying for people when I told them I would) or physical (e.g., skipping workouts).

The more I studied this out, the more links I discovered between complacency and these other concepts. Self-satisfaction and pride, for instance, are my primary struggle when I'm seeing progress in a weight loss program—but that's when I begin to feel *entitled* to reward myself.

Laziness also happens to be a fruit of complacency. And complacency is listed as a related word to apathy.

This lifelong struggle finally made sense.

> *So, if you think you are standing firm, be careful that you don't fall!*
>
> — 1 CORINTHIANS 10:12 (NIV)

The Lord led me to 2 Kings 18, to a story about King Hezekiah. Hezekiah did what was pleasing to the Lord. He smashed the pagan alters and removed the shrines. He trusted in God, and he even rebelled against the king of Assyria.

The Assyrians were wicked, so this was a good type of rebellion—the way I should rebel against the temptation to eat junk food or surf social media.

But as Hezekiah's reign continued, something shifted. The Bible doesn't say what, specifically, but his behavior

THE COMPLACENCY TRAP

parallels my own. He started off zealous and full of faith, then his zeal waned. After Assyria captured Samaria in the Northern Kingdom, Hezekiah—in the Southern Kingdom—acquiesced to Assyria's demands, offering to pay whatever tribute was demanded of him.

Hezekiah gave up. He quit fighting, and in that moment he didn't trust the Lord to deliver him but instead relied on his own strength. He paid the tribute, and guess how he did it? With all the silver from the Temple of the Lord. The Bible even says that Hezekiah stripped the gold from the doorposts.

Reading this, I realized I do this very thing. When stress is high and my faith is low, what are the first things I abandon? Not social media. Not junk food. Instead, I give up the precious spiritual things in my life—fasting, reading my Bible, spending time with God.

That gold and silver were not Hezekiah's to give. They belonged to the Lord. Likewise, when I give up the spiritual things in my life, those are not mine to give. They belong to the Lord, because my life belongs to Him.

> *I have been crucified with Christ and I no longer live, but Christ lives in me. The life I now live in the body, I live by faith in the Son of God, who loved me and gave himself for me.*
>
> — GALATIANS 2:20 (NIV)

The most dangerous sins are those that seem harmless. Complacency is one of those sins, because I can always justify it. It's *just* one piece of cake. It's *just* skipping one devotion time. It's *just* a quick break from reading my Bible.

Just.

Just.

Just.

I like to think I'm doing well spiritually, but Scripture shines light on how bad complacency and its underpinnings really are. Complacency, as it turns out, was one of Sodom's sins.

> *"'Now this was the iniquity of your sister Sodom: She and her daughters were arrogant, overfed and unconcerned; they did not help the poor and needy.'"*
>
> — EZEKIEL 16:49 (NIV)

If that wasn't enough, Jesus addressed apathy (related to complacency) in Matthew 25 through the Parable of the Talents. In that parable, He called the apathetic servant "wicked and lazy," and He banished that servant to outer darkness.

Many people—believers and unbelievers alike, even entire nations—suffer from various forms of complacency. This sin manifests in different ways, to different degrees, but God loves us and desires to deliver us from this trap. Repentance is the key, because it activates the blood of Jesus.

> *"Repent, then, and turn to God, so that your sins may be wiped out, that times of refreshing may come from the Lord."*
>
> — ACTS 3:19 (NIV)

The Prayer of Saint Ephrem is a beautiful prayer of repentance from the fourth century that speaks of these same things. The struggle is real, and it's been happening for a really long time (since the beginning).

THE COMPLACENCY TRAP

If you struggle with complacency like I do, let's ask God for the grace to turn from our sin and receive His freedom....

O Lord and Master of my life, take from me a spirit of despondency, sloth, love of power, and idle talk. But give to me, your servant, a spirit of sober-mindedness, humility, patience, and love. Yes, O Lord and King, grant me to see my own sins and not to judge my brother, since you are blessed to the ages of ages. Amen.

25
RHYME & REASON
WEDNESDAY

Sometimes there's rhyme and reason behind the madness...
and sometimes there's not. That's okay. God is sovereign.

WAS PAUL REALLY A CHAUVINIST?

Was Paul really a chauvinist as many feminists say?

> *But every woman who prays or prophesies with her head uncovered dishonors her head—it is the same as having her head shaved. For if a woman does not cover her head, she might as well have her hair cut off; but if it is a disgrace for a woman to have her hair cut off or her head shaved, then she should cover her head.*
>
> — 1 CORINTHIANS 11:5-6 (NIV)

First Corinthians Thirteen is called the "love chapter." It's where the Bible talks about faith, hope, and love. It's where we're taught the definition of love (love is patient, love is kind). But what about the rest of First Corinthians?

In the next chapter, Paul declared that women should

keep silent in church (1 COR 14:34). A few chapters back, he commanded women on how to wear their hair (1 COR 11:5). Secular humanists often condemn these verses, calling Paul a chauvinist and a hypocrite.

I must admit, it seems a bit odd. How could a man, who wrote such profound things about love in chapter thirteen, be so critical in other chapters?

I've heard Bible scholars talk about Corinth and how the church was experiencing problems, some of which may have included mid-service disruptions. Makes sense, but it doesn't explain the verses about women's hair. Paul puts emphasis on this for a reason, but why? Is it really a sin for women to have short hair?

Two years ago, I joined my church on a biblical studies tour of Greece. One of our stops was none other than Corinth. Ancient stone pillars and Roman ruins scattered the archeological site. Acrocorinth (a mountain and monolithic rock) overlooked the city.

"What's that?" I asked, pointing at a fortress-type structure atop Acrocorinth.

"That is where the Temple of Aphrodite resided," our tour guide said.

He went on to explain that the Aphrodite worshipers, many of whom were sex slaves, wore their heads shaved. Culturally, it was a mark of identity. But as the Gospel spread, many of these women found a new identity in Christ.

"What do you think would happen," our tour guide asked, "when a woman with a shaved head arrived in the church? Her past, her sin, was on display for the congregation, because her hair did not grow out overnight."

All have sinned, all have fallen short of the glory of God... but what if we had to walk around with our past sin on full display? What if the idolatry we'd been steeped in before Christ was obvious to the world long after our salvation experience—not because we willfully shared our testimony, but because people could simply look at us (daily) and see what we'd been doing in the darkness?

Now imagine the nature of *that* particular sin. These were women who broke up marriages. They slept with other women's husbands, brothers, fathers. Their job was to cause people to stumble, and although many received the Gospel and repented—although they became new creations in Christ—they still carried the mark of their past.

A mark of shame.

As head of the church, Paul knew what it cost to receive these women as members of the congregation—and there was, in fact, a cost in addition to the metaphoric or spiritual kind. Many of these sex slaves had to be purchased (redeemed) from their life of bondage. For the women who became Christians, a wealthy member of the church often acted as the redeemer and purchased their freedom.

"What then?" our guide asked. "These women would go to church, repentant and anew, yet they had to continue bearing this old shame."

His explanation painted these verses in a whole new light. I finally understood—when Paul referred to short hair as shameful, he was referring to the mark of shame these former Aphrodite worshipers carried. Even if these women tried to cover their heads, other Christians would see the difference. People would know, with but a glance, the sinful past of these women. Paul knew this could cause division, hurt feelings, and even animosity.

So Paul instructed the other women to cover their heads, too. For the sake of love.

 "Greater love has no one than this: to lay down one's life for one's friends."

— JOHN 15:13 (NIV)

Paul explained that a woman's long hair was beautiful, her "glory," but in love—at least during church services—he wanted the women to lay that glory aside. By doing so, it would no longer be *just* the former Aphrodite worshipers covering their heads. It would be all the women, united as sisters, because love does...what?

Paul gives us the answer two chapters later.

> *Love is patient, love is kind . . . . it does not boast, it is not proud. It does not dishonor others, it is not self-seeking . . . . it keeps no record of wrongs . . . . It always protects, always trusts, always hopes, always perseveres.*
>
> — 1 CORINTHIANS 13:4-6 (NIV)

The apostle Peter put it this way.

> *Above all, love each other deeply, because love covers over a multitude of sins.*
>
> — 1 PETER 4:8 (NIV)

Secular humanists look at the Bible and say it's full of hatred, violence. The carnal mind cannot accept that the Bible is about love, but it is. The Scriptures teach about God's love for us, and it teaches us how to love others (and Him) in a fallen world. God *is* love. He's *agape*—a willful, self-sacrificing love.

The highest form of love.

If it seems like Paul was asking the women of Corinth to

sacrifice something by covering their heads—well, it's because he was. For the sake of love. Let this be our prayer: that all we do would be done in love, even if it means sacrificing something of ourselves in the process.

 And now these three remain: faith, hope and love. But the greatest of these is love.

— 1 CORINTHIANS 13:13 (NIV)

26
IS THURSDAY A TERSE DAY?

Are you having a rough week? I hope not, but in case you are, don't forget the Holy Spirit's encouragement...

YOU ARE MORE

I had a meltdown at a bus station in Lima, Peru.

> ***There's a girl in the corner***
> ***With tear stains on her eyes***
> ***From the places she's wandered***
> ***And the shame she can't hide***

— TENTH AVENUE NORTH

When I gave my life to Christ, I signed up for a mission trip called the World Race where I would live in eleven countries over the course of eleven months. One of those countries was Peru.

I felt whole and complete as a new Christian, with the peace of the Lord in my heart and mind. So, of course, that led me to believe the depression had miraculously gone away.

It hadn't, and there were times when the depression showed up intensely, particularly when I was under stress.

One such instance happened when my squad and I were traveling from Peru to our next country, Ecuador.

One of the great (and hard) things about long-term missions is how far outside our comfort zone we might find ourselves at any given time. God uses these types of things to refine us, stretching us to the breaking point.

He didn't do it to be mean. He did it because I needed it, and He loves me enough to take me through the process. But when I broke in Peru, I broke hard. I failed to lean on Him, to rest in His Strength, and I crumbled.

> *"Imagine yourself as a living house. God comes in to rebuild that house."*
>
> — C.S. LEWIS

Even though my life became radically different after I met Jesus—even though I had changed in very real, very noticeable ways—that didn't mean all my problems went away.

The Lord has had a ton of issues to work through in me, and teaching me to break agreement with shame and depression, to wage war against sin, has encompassed a mere fraction of the battle. It hasn't been easy, and I came close to calling it quits several times.

It's too hard! I would cry out in my heart, and even aloud during heartfelt prayer. *I can't do it anymore!*

But each time I said "I can't do this," He would counter that lie with: YOU CAN. Sometimes I believed Him. Sometimes I didn't.

> *"When we come to the end of ourselves, we come to the beginning of God."*
>
> — BILLY GRAHAM

It was seven in the morning when I broke in Lima, Peru. I was sitting at the bus station, waiting to climb aboard the bus that would take my squad to Ecuador.

As I sat there, silent tears pouring, all I could think about was how badly I always messed everything up. I started criticizing myself, taking myself down a destructive path of self-condemnation.

Shame bubbled up from deep inside my heart. My thoughts spiraled, sliding deeper into a dark chasm I hadn't realized still existed in me.

Cheeks moist, I tipped my head back and closed my teary eyes. Supernatural peace overshadowed me, then He showed me a vision I'll never forget—Jesus on the Cross.

My heart swelled. The tears that fell next weren't for me. They were for my Hero, my Savior, the One who chose to suffer so that I could be free.

As the reminder of Christ's sacrifice unfolded before me, the gut-wrenching heartache I had been feeling died away. It died right there on the Cross. He took it. He bought my suffering with His own. I had no choice but to turn it over to Him.

> *Jesus has borne the death penalty on our behalf. Behold the wonder! . . . . Son of God and Son of Man, there He hangs, bearing pains unutterable, the just for the unjust, to bring us to God."*
>
> — CHARLES SPURGEON

I often wonder what people think when they hear, "Jesus loves you." The concept of love has become so warped in our world, and I don't even think people can understand what it means for Jesus to love us. I certainly didn't.

After I chose to follow Christ, it took a long time to

comprehend that God could love us so wholly, even through our rejection of Him, even through our deepest, darkest sins.

But He loved us first. He loved us when we hated him. It's His nature. He loves like no one else because He isn't like anyone else. That's why He sent His Holy Spirit to live in those who have repented of their sins and have chosen to trust in Christ, to advocate for us and convict us.

And, in this case, to comfort us.

Whenever I'm struggling, it seems like the Holy Spirit highlights certain songs. When I was on mission, after that crazy experience in Lima, He highlighted a song called "You Are More" by Tenth Avenue North. The lyrics explore the pain and heartache sin brings, but also the hope we have in Jesus.

"This is not about what you've done," the singer says, "but what's been done for you." And later, "This is not about what you feel, but what He's done to forgive you."

The song is a reminder of God's great love and everything He's done to redeem me to Himself. It reminds me that I'm seen and loved, but also that I'm not the focal point (He is) and to lift my gaze higher.

I'm *more* than the choices I've made.

I'm *more* than the sum of my past mistakes.

I'm *more* than the problems I create.

Because I've been REMADE... and you have, too.

Therefore, if anyone is in Christ, the new creation has come: The old has gone, the new is here!

— 2 CORINTHIANS 5:17 (NIV)

❧ 27 ❧
FRIDAY NO-CRY DAY

"There's no crying in baseball!"

— JIMMY DUGAN'S CHARACTER (PLAYED BY TOM HANKS) IN 'A LEAGUE OF THEIR OWN'

A BRUISED REED

There was a time when I would workout for hours, with my iPod blasting, running as hard as I can, while listening to a playlist full of my favorite praise and worship songs.

One day while I was doing just such a workout, I realized I had time to squeeze in a little strength training at the end, and I decided to do calf-raises on a sturdy cement block. The block was small, the ideal height, and perfectly positioned beside a small tree, which I gripped to keep my balance.

But as I was doing the exercise, I found myself with a thin-but-leafy tree branch right in my face. I swatted at it, pushing it down until it bent and broke—well, sort of broke. It didn't fully break off, but it was out of the way enough to finish my calf-raises.

About a week later, I was at the same park, doing the same calf-raises. The branch was still there, still hanging and halfway broken. But unlike before when all the leaves were nice and green, the branch was dead, the leaves brown and crispy.

I surveyed the rest of the tree. It was green and healthy. Only that one branch had wilted.

> *A bruised reed he will not break, and a smoldering wick he will not snuff out.*
>
> — ISAIAH 42:3(A) (NIV)

A paused and let the Holy Spirit minister to me, reflecting on this verse about the bruised reed, which someone had just shared with me. And as I observed that dead branch, the realization hit me—I had done that. Me. I caused that branch to become damaged and wilted.

It was a very normal, very human thing to do—if something's bothering you, you deal with it whatever way is most appropriate by: by moving it, getting around it, setting it aside.

And if you *can't* get around it—if you are determined to have this thing out of your way, but it's not moving—what do you do?

You break through it.

I hadn't thought about the consequences of my actions up until that point. It was just a branch, and a small one at that. It wasn't even a main branch of the tree, just a skinny offshoot. Nothing that affected the tree as a whole—but the longer I stared at that brown, crispy, dead branch, in such contrast to the green branches, the Holy Spirit's message dawned.

This is what we do, to each other, through selfishness and sin. We damage pieces of their hearts (and also our own). Our sin may be unintentional (I didn't intend to damage the branch; I really just wanted it out of the way), but the damage occurred nonetheless.

This is how God differs so vastly from us. And this was the ultimate epiphany I had.

Instead of breaking a branch that was troubling Him, He would have dug up the entire tree, roots and all, and then replanted it in a better spot. All the roots would have been delicately handled. All the branches would have been maintained. The tree would be in one healthy piece by the time He was done with it.

He would have taken greater care. He would have been more delicate. That's how He deals with us.

God's solutions aren't always immediate. Oftentimes we assume He isn't working because we're not seeing results. But that's because He's picking out the perfect spot for us, and He's carefully digging up our roots, and carefully replanting us.

He's concerned with doing the process right. Not doing it *fast*.

Don't get me wrong. When He wants to move things along, He can have a whole grove of trees replanted immediately. But a lot of times, He's focused on how the process will benefit us, what we'll learn from it.

I believe He takes pleasure in this process, and it's mind-blowing to think that the Living God, Creator of Heaven and Earth, cares about us so deeply that He would take such time and care and be so tender with us.

All glory to the Master Gardner, who prunes and trims and refines those who belong to Him, the One who delights in all His creation. All blessings, honor, and power to the Lamb who sits on the throne forever. Amen.

> *"Here is my servant, whom I uphold,*
> *my chosen one in whom I delight;*
> *I will put my Spirit on him,*
> *and he will bring justice to the nations.*

He will not shout or cry out,
or raise his voice in the streets.
A bruised reed he will not break,
and a smoldering wick he will not snuff out.
In faithfulness he will bring forth justice;
he will not falter or be discouraged
till he establishes justice on earth.
In his teaching the islands will put their hope."

— ISAIAH 42:1-4

28
SATURDAY MUSING

Another Saturday musing (just in case you need it)...

TRUE LOVE

Love is heartache
Love is rhyme
Not so lovely
All the time
Love will make you
Sad today
Tomorrow's joy
Is marked by pain
Sorrows multiply
The truth
Happiness
A fleeting fruit
But this one thing
I know for sure
The truest love
It shall endure

— K.M. ELLIS

29
ONE LAST SUNDAY

Technically, this is a bonus day. But Sunday *is* a bonus, so....

ALL THAT SAVES

A warm wind blows
Her warm-blonde hair
Waving, washing
If you dare
A wave that washes
Over me
A pale black night
A memory
A scent that makes it
All come back
A warmth that crushes
Tit-for-tat
A surge that brushes
'Gainst her mind
That rushes through
The sands of time
And in that moment
Stillness reigns
A Savior's love
Is all that saves

OLD WHINE, NEW WINE

— K.M. ELLIS

❧ 30 ☙
A FINAL MONDAY

We can always use a little extra encouragement on Monday...

THE KING'S GATE

J ust because God calls you TO a door doesn't mean He's calling you *through* it.

> *When Mordecai learned of all that had been done [Haman's plot against the Jews], he tore his clothes, put on sackcloth and ashes, and went out into the city, wailing loudly and bitterly. But he went only as far as the king's gate, because no one clothed in sackcloth was allowed to enter it.*
>
> — ESTHER 4:1-2 (NIV)

Immediately after a prayer call one morning, while I was still praying, I pictured myself trying to push my way through an open door. But I realized it was open for others (not me). Then saw myself sitting by the door, praying, warring in the Spirit, as others walked through that same door freely.

Mordecai came to mind. I looked up the story, and sure enough, he was stationed at the king's gate. He actually accomplished a lot just sitting there. He fasted, he wept, he prayed and put ashes on his head...but what he did *not* do was go through that gate.

That was Esther's job. She was the one called to go to the king. Mordecai was called to unveil the enemy's plans, and he did - then he supported Esther through intercession.

She did her job. He did his.

We all have unique callings, and we may be called to something different in each seasons. It's critical we follow the leadership of the Holy Spirit so that we know what God is calling us to now, in this hour, in this season. Because even if we're not being called *through* a door, we could be called to be stationed *at* that door (like Mordecai was stationed at the king's gate) to pray, fast, and otherwise support those who are in fact being called through it.

We may not necessarily think Mordecai's position was as important as Esther's, but what he did may very well have waged the spiritual violence (i.e., spiritual warfare) needed to advance God's Kingdom and ultimately rescue God's people in Persia.

Let's pray.

God, thank You for the gift of prayer. There may be seasons where we're called to go, but there may also be seasons where we're called to stay and pray. May our prayers be as powerful as those of Mordecai's, affecting lives and even entire nations, and may we never forget that prayer is the most powerful thing we can ever do. In Jesus' name. Amen.

BONUS: SNEAK PEEK OF BOOK #2

Keep reading for a sneak peek of *Toil to Oil: Book of Encouragement, #2*...

TWO WRONGS

If someone wrongs us, even in some horrific way, it doesn't give us legal permission to take the law into our own hands.

It's not *legal* to murder someone because they slept with our spouse.

It's not *legal* to steal someone's house because they gossiped about you.

If we respond to someone's transgression with another transgression—even if what that person did was wrong, even if what they did was illegal—*you* are the one who could very well end up in court. You might even go to jail, especially if you took the law into our own hands.

Vigilante justice isn't really justice. It's just a way for someone to circumvent the legal system and issue their own brand of justice.

In the same way, we cannot take up our own spiritual vengeance. We cannot avenge ourselves by murdering someone's character or attacking them with vicious words and gossip, threats of violence or manipulation.

If they're guilty, let them be found guilty! We must not join them in their guilt.

> "You have heard that it was said, 'Eye for eye, and tooth for tooth.' But I say to you, Do not resist the one who is evil. But if anyone slaps you on the right cheek, turn to him the other also."
>
> — MATTHEW 5:38-39 (ESV)

> "You have heard that it was said, 'You shall love your neighbor and hate your enemy.' But I say to you, Love your enemies and pray for those who persecute you,"
>
> — MATTHEW 5:43-44 (ESV)

Jesus didn't say these things because He was promoting injustice. On the contrary, Jesus was teaching us how to keep our hearts right before God and to give us a process for dealing with the hurt people will inevitably inflict upon us.

Forgiveness doesn't excuse other people's behavior. It doesn't give them a verdict of "not guilty" in God's court. Rather, forgiveness keeps *us* from being found guilty instead.

Let God vindicate you. Leave justice in the hands of Him that administers perfect justice. Some people may get away with murder (literally) on this side of eternity, but they will *never* escape God's wrath and justice on the other side.

There will be a time when all of mankind's ugly secrets are revealed. GUARANTEED. So keep on forgiving. Then you'll have a clear conscience today and forevermore.

THE PLIGHT OF MANKIND

The reason sin—even one sin—is enough to condemn people to hell is that one sin can have yearslong consequences in other people's lives, extending beyond that person's life and into the lives of those around them. That sin can keep going, keep repeating, until it even extends into the next generations.

I look back at the bullying I was subjected to as a child, third grade through junior high, and I feel sure I don't remember every single thing everyone did to me. But I know there are at least a dozen classmates whose words or actions (perhaps on only on one or two occasions) tormented me into my adulthood.

And it didn't stop there. The torment followed me into my sleep life, my dreams, and became recurring nightmares I've battled my whole life. The scars have affected countless friendships, jobs, volunteer activities, my ability to communicate, my ability to relate to others. Even to this day, it affects my marriage.

The consequences of other people's sin has spilled over into just about every facet of my life. Thankfully, I've found healing in some of those areas, and I know Christ will bring me through the rest, but what about all those years of damage that happened before I knew Him? What about all the relationships ruined? The precious moments stolen from me, which I'll never get back? What about the hurt in God's heart because I now have trust issues with *Him*?

Don't misunderstand me. God is trustworthy. I know that. But the warped layers of brokenness in my heart prevent me from fully believing that He is righteous and just and good. Why? Because bullying marred my emotions and created a warped lens through which I see everything and everyone.

I was processing through a lot of these things today, and I realized... we may not be asking the right questions. Because it's not a matter of: "How can a good God send people to hell?"

Actually, it's more like: "How could a good God NOT send people to hell?" Because our sin can have lifelong consequences on other people. One single sin can change the course of someone's life. And the truth is, in our carnal nature, we really are sinning in some way perpetually, almost without stopping.

> *The LORD saw that the wickedness of man was great in the earth, and that every intention of the thoughts of his heart was only evil continually.*
>
> — GENESIS 6:5 (NIV)

> *Now when he was in Jerusalem at the Passover Feast, many believed in his name when they saw the signs that he was doing. But Jesus on his part did not entrust himself to them, because he knew all people and needed*

no one to bear witness about man, for he himself knew what was in man.

— JOHN 2:23-25 (NIV)

 For whatever does not proceed from faith is sin.

— ROMANS 14:23 (NIV)

Every selfish or self-focused action is sin... but also every selfish or self-focused *thought* or *intention*.

We want to believe that human beings are mostly good, but if we look at the world at large, what do we see? Betrayal, sabotage, gossip, manipulation, control, power grabs, violence, injustice.

Such atrocities can be found everywhere. Many have happened to me. Many have probably happened to you. No one is immune from the outworking of mankind's corrupted (fallen) nature...

And yet, He cares for us. May God have mercy on us all.

A MUCH-NEEDED REMINDER

Repeat after me…

I am not forgotten. I'm remembered.
I am not unloved. I'm cherished.
I am not a burden. I'm a blessing.
I am not rejected. I'm accepted in the Beloved.
I am not unprotected. I'm protected. I'm watched over. I'm cared for by GOD.

THE GIFT

I'm a broken mess
A wreck
Cracked in half by sinking sand
I can't do this anymore
Rejection stings as I run out the door
Like a punch in the gut
Or a slap in the face
I'm down, I'm injured
I'm out of this race
And I don't know if I'll ever go back
I'm not sure I'm able
I'm not sure I can
Because I make things a hundred times worse
This gift of mine... it's a blessing and a curse

— K.M. ELLIS

ABOUT THE AUTHOR

Most of the time, you'll find K.M. Ellis reading, writing, or praying (or some combination of these). Sometimes you might find her traveling. She and her husband love Jesus, their families, their friends, and their sweet doggos.

www.ingramcontent.com/pod-product-compliance
Lightning Source LLC
LaVergne TN
LVHW041229080426
835508LV00011B/1120